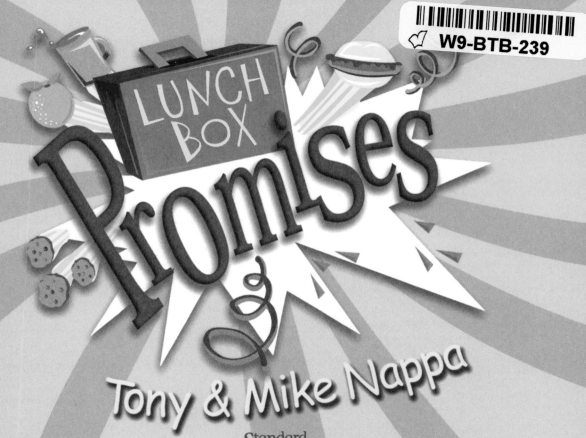

LUNCH BOX Promises

Tony & Mike Nappa

Standard
Publishing
Cincinnati, Ohio

W9-BTB-239

For Grampa Norm, whose love of Scripture inspires us all.

Standard Publishing, a division of Standex International Corporation, Cincinnati, Ohio.
© 2000 by Nappaland Communications, Inc. All rights reserved.
Bean Sprouts™ and the Bean Sprouts design logo are trademarks of Standard Publishing.
Printed in the United States of America.
Design: Diana Walters. Typesetting: Andrew Quach.

07 06 05 04 03 02 01 00   5 4 3 2 1

ISBN 0-7847-1181-X

Scripture quotations marked NIV are taken from the HOLY BIBLE, NEW INTERNATIONAL VERSION®. NIV®. Copyright © 1973, 1978, 1984 by the International Bible Society. Used by permission of Zondervan Publishing House. All rights reserved.

Scripture quotations marked NLT are taken from the *Holy Bible, New Living Translation,* copyright © 1996. Used by permission of Tyndale House Publishers, Inc., Wheaton, Illinois 60189. All rights reserved.

Scripture quotations marked CEV are taken from *The New Testament of the Contemporary English Version,* copyright © The American Bible Society 1995. Published under license from Thomas Nelson Publishers. Used by permission.

Scripture quotations marked NCV are taken from *The Youth Bible, New Century Version,* copyright © 1991 by Word Publishing, Dallas, Texas 75039. Used by permission.

Scripture quotations marked NKJV are taken from the *New King James Version*. Copyright © 1979, 1980, 1982 by Thomas Nelson, Inc. Used by permission. All rights reserved.

Scripture quotation on back cover from the *International Children's Bible, New Century Version,* copyright © 1986, 1988 by Word Publishing, Dallas, Texas 75039. Used by permission.

Lunch Box Promises is another creative resource from the authors at Nappaland Communications, Inc. You can contact the authors through their web site at www.Nappaland.com

A Note to Parents

I love this book—and not just because I got to help in the writing of it. I love it because coauthoring it with my nine-year-old son, Tony, caused us to plunge ourselves deep into the pages of Scripture. For days at a time, Tony and I found ourselves reading and discussing the Word of God and how it applies to our lives. I discovered that Psalm 23 is my son's favorite Bible passage. And I discovered that he still remembers the details of Bible stories we read to him as a preschooler!

I love this book also because it reminds me of the life-changing power of God, of my desperate need for him, and because it provides once again the reassurance that God does indeed love and care for me and my son. How do I know? The Bible tells me so.

Which brings me to the purpose for this book. As a parent, I want to plant the Word of God within my son's heart, to give him that source of faith and strength to guide him through the rest of his life. I'm betting you want to do that, too. And that's why Tony and I have put together *Lunch Box Promises: Over 75 Tear-Out Notes With Promises From God's Word*. We've collected our favorite Bible verses and put them in here with the hope that you'll pass them on to your children as well.

You'll notice that the pages in this book are perforated. That's because we figured the next time you're packing a child's lunch, you might have a sudden urge to tear out a Bible promise from this book and slip it in with the juice box and bag of chips. When your youngster opens her lunch at school later that day, she will be treated to an encouraging word from the Scriptures to keep in mind for the rest of the afternoon. And you'll be treated to the satisfaction of knowing you planted a bit of God's Word in your child's day. Our prayer is that this book will encourage your family as much as we were encouraged by putting it together for you.

So what are you waiting for? Isn't it time to pack a lunch?

Mike Nappa, 1999

God's Promise

"Be strong and of good courage, do not fear nor be afraid . . . for the Lord your God, He is the One who goes with you. He will not leave you nor forsake you."

Deuteronomy 31:6 (NKJV)

What Does This Mean For Me?

God is the most powerful force in the universe and he promises to help you face any trouble in life–always!

God's Promise

"Everything in the Scriptures is God's Word. All of it is useful for teaching and helping people and for correcting them and showing them how to live."

2 Timothy 3:16 (CEV)

What Does This Mean For Me?

God has given you a great gift—the Bible! You can trust what the Bible says, knowing it will help you live for God every day of your life.

God's Promise

"Look! Here I stand at the door and knock. If you hear me calling and open the door, I will come in, and we will share a meal as friends."
Revelation 3:20 (NLT)

What Does This Mean For Me?

Jesus made this promise to you because he wants to be your best friend! He waits each day for you to pray and talk to him—so why not pray to him right now?

God's Promise

"Be of good courage, and He
[God] shall strengthen your
heart, all you who hope in
the Lord."
Psalm 31:24 (NKJV)

What Does This Mean For Me?

When you feel like giving up, you can ask God for strength to keep going—and he will help you!

God's Promise

"Come near to God, and he will come near to you."

James 4:8 (CEV)

What Does This Mean For Me?

God is always nearby! And when you spend time reading the Bible, praying, or obeying God, you can grow even closer to him!

God's Promise

"For I can do everything with the help of Christ who gives me the strength I need."
Philippians 4:13 (NLT)

What Does This Mean For Me?

With Jesus as your helper, you can do anything you have to do—whether it's standing up to temptation or finishing that really hard math assignment!

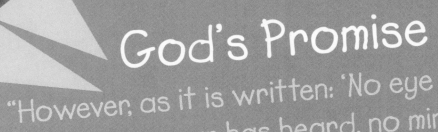

God's Promise

"However, as it is written: 'No eye has seen, no ear has heard, no mind has conceived what God has prepared for those who love him.'"
1 Corinthians 2:9 (NIV)

What Does This Mean For Me?

God has great things in store for you—including (best of all) a brand new relationship with Jesus Christ, his Son!

God's Promise

"for every child of God defeats this evil world by trusting Christ to give the victory."
1 John 5:4 (NLT)

What Does This Mean For Me?

Sometimes it may be hard to follow God. Friends may make fun of you, or you might be tempted to do something you know is wrong. At those times, you can ask Jesus to help you, and he will give you strength to follow God no matter what!

God's Promise

"God shows his great love for us in this way: Christ died for us while we were still sinners."

Romans 5:8 (NCV)

What Does This Mean For Me?

God loves you—and he proved it! Even before you knew God existed, he allowed Jesus to die on the cross to pay the penalty for your wrongs.

God's Promise

"Even though I walk through the valley of the shadow of death, I will fear no evil, for you are with me." Psalm 23:4 (NIV)

What Does This Mean For Me?

Here's a news flash: Life isn't easy! (You knew that already, huh?) But you don't have to be worried or afraid. God promises that he will always be right by your side, going with you through any hard time you face.

God's Promise

"Do you not know? Have you not heard? The Lord is the everlasting God, the Creator of the ends of the earth. He will not grow tired or weary."
Isaiah 40:28 (NIV)

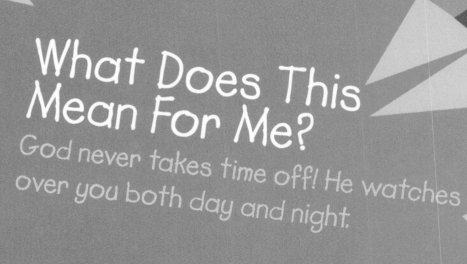

What Does This Mean For Me?

God never takes time off! He watches over you both day and night.

God's Promise

"The Lord will give strength to His people; The Lord will bless His people with peace."
Psalm 29:11 (NKJV)

What Does This Mean For Me?

God loves his people and he loves to give them good things like strength and peace.

God's Promise

"We are certain that God will hear our prayers when we ask for what pleases him." 1 John 5:14 (CEV)

What Does This Mean For Me?

God listens to your prayers! So pray for things you know God wants! If you're not sure what God wants, read the Bible to find out!

God's Promise

"Those who become Christians become new persons. They are not the same anymore, for the old life is gone. A new life has begun!"
2 Corinthians 5:17 (NLT)

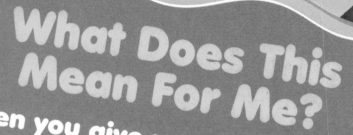

What Does This Mean For Me?

When you give your life to Jesus, he forgives all the wrong things you've ever done and helps you become like him.

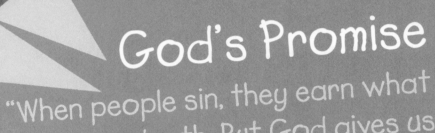

God's Promise

"When people sin, they earn what sin pays—death. But God gives us a free gift—life forever in Christ Jesus our Lord."

Romans 6:23 (NCV)

What Does This Mean For Me?

Doing wrong things is called sinning. Sin leads to death forever. But Jesus can forgive all our sins and give us life forever in heaven instead!

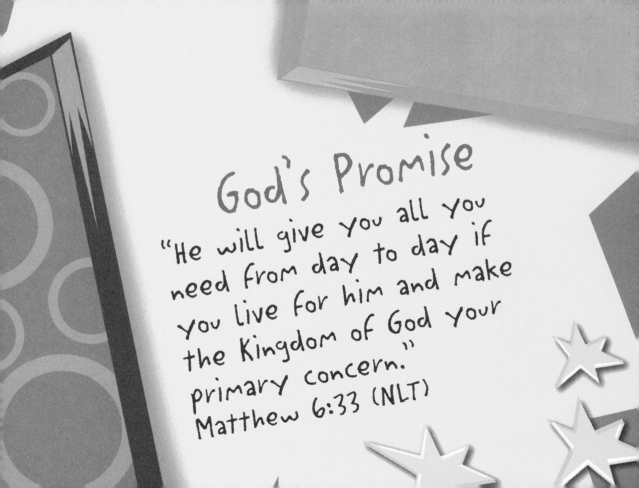

God's Promise

"He will give you all you need from day to day if you live for him and make the Kingdom of God your primary concern."

Matthew 6:33 (NLT)

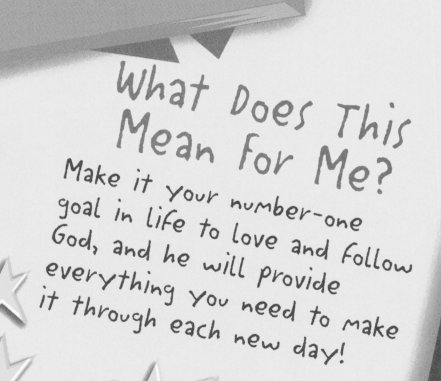

What Does This Mean For Me?

Make it your number-one goal in life to love and follow God, and he will provide everything you need to make it through each new day!

God's Promise

"Honor your father and mother. Then you will live a long, full life in the land the Lord your God will give you." Exodus 20:12 (NLT)

What Does This Mean For Me?

Sure, they get on your nerves sometimes, but God gave you parents as a special gift to help you through life. Obey your parents. Treat them with respect and kindness, and God will reward you for that.

God's Promise

"I will make you wise and show you where to go. I will guide you and watch over you."

Psalm 32:8 (NCV)

What Does This Mean For Me?

When you feel confused and unsure of what is right or wrong, ask God for help! He has given you the Bible to help you, and it's a great place to start when you're looking for God's guidance.

God's Promise

"'For I know the plans I have for you,' says the Lord. 'They are plans for good and not for disaster, to give you a future and a hope.'"

Jeremiah 29:11 (NLT)

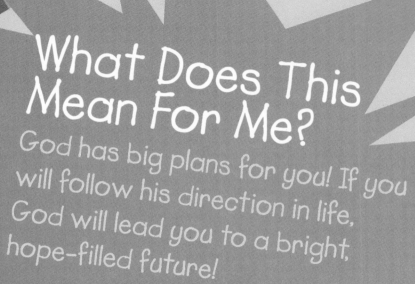

What Does This Mean For Me?

God has big plans for you! If you will follow his direction in life, God will lead you to a bright, hope-filled future!

God's Promise

"My God will use his wonderful riches in Christ Jesus to give you everything you need."
Philippians 4:19 (NCV)

What Does This Mean For Me?

It's true you may not always have everything you want, but God promises to give you all you need in life. That's a relief, huh?

God's Promise

"I trust in God. I will not be afraid. What can people do to me?"

Psalm 56:11 (NCV)

What Does This Mean For Me?

It's true that people can sometimes hurt you. But when you trust in God, you don't have to be afraid of what people can do to you because you know that in the end, God will always watch over you!

God's Promise

"The Lord won't leave his people nor give up his children." Psalm 94:14 (NCV)

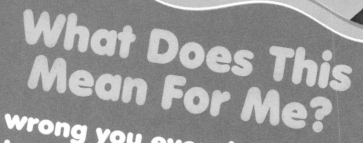

What Does This Mean For Me?

No wrong you ever do will make God so mad that he gives up on you. He loves you and promises to be with you.

God's Promise

"For I am the Lord, your God, who takes hold of your right hand and says to you, Do not fear; I will help you." Isaiah 41:13 (NIV)

What Does This Mean For Me?

God, the one who created everything in the universe, cares about *you*. He will always be near to you, and will help you in times of trouble.

God's Promise

"I will answer them before they even call to me. While they are still talking to me about their needs, I will go ahead and answer their prayers!"
Isaiah 65:24 (NLT)

What Does This Mean For Me?

God hears every prayer, and he answers every prayer, too. God is so amazing that he even knows what we need before we ask it!

God's Promise

"I love you people with a love that will last forever. That is why I have continued showing you kindness."

Jeremiah 31:3 (NCV)

What Does This Mean For Me?

God loves you, both now and forever!

God's Promise

"The steps of the godly are directed by the Lord. He delights in every detail of their lives."
Psalm 37:23 (NLT)

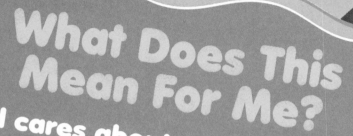

What Does This Mean For Me?

God cares about everything that happens in your life. You can pray to him and read the Bible to find direction for your life.

God's Promise

"And I am sure that God, who began the good work within you, will continue his work until it is finally finished on that day when Christ Jesus comes back again."
Philippians 1:6 (NLT)

What Does This Mean For Me?

You are one of God's very special projects, and every day for the rest of your life God will help you become more and more like Jesus!

God's Promise

"The Lord is good, a refuge in times of trouble. He cares for those who trust in him."
Nahum 1:7 (NIV)

What Does This Mean For Me?

God is good! He will care for you as you trust him to supply your needs each day.

God's Promise

"Give your worries to the Lord, and he will take care of you. He will never let good people down."

Psalm 55:22 (NCV)

What Does This Mean For Me?

Do you worry about your grades, or your family, or your future? Next time you feel like worrying, tell God about your concerns instead, and then trust in him to care for you.

God's Promise

"For God has not given us a spirit of fear, but of power and of love and of a sound mind."
2 Timothy 1:7 (NKJV)

What Does This Mean For Me?

Don't be afraid to tell your friends about Jesus. God gives us strength, love, and good sense to help us.

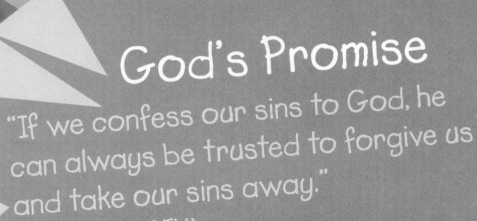

God's Promise

"If we confess our sins to God, he can always be trusted to forgive us and take our sins away."
1 John 1:9 (CEV)

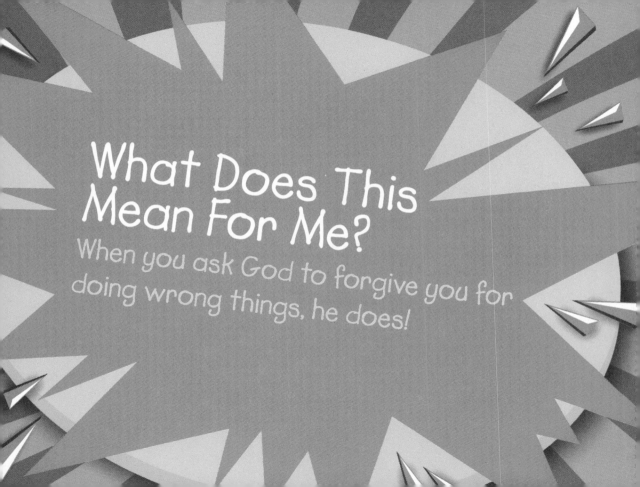

What Does This Mean For Me?

When you ask God to forgive you for doing wrong things, he does!

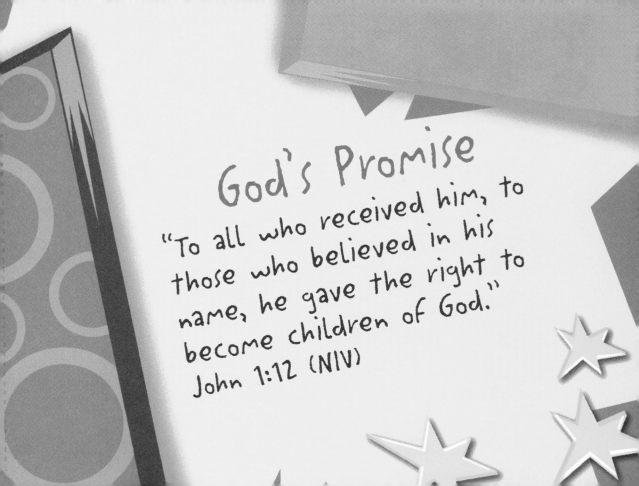

God's Promise

"To all who received him, to
those who believed in his
name, he gave the right to
become children of God."
John 1:12 (NIV)

What Does This Mean For Me?

God promises that when you believe in Jesus, you can become part of his family! God will "adopt" you as his child.

God's Promise

"No matter how deep the stain of your sins, I can remove it. I can make you as clean as freshly fallen snow. Even if you are stained as red as crimson, I can make you as white as wool."

Isaiah 1:18 (NLT)

What Does This Mean For Me?

No matter how bad your sins may be, if you ask God to forgive you, he will. He will treat you as though you've never done anything wrong at all.

God's Promise

"For this is God, our God forever and ever; He will be our guide even to death."
Psalm 48:14 (NKJV)

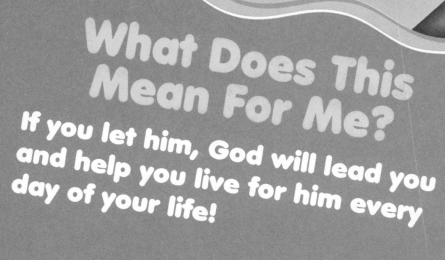

What Does This Mean For Me?

If you let him, God will lead you and help you live for him every day of your life!

God's Promise

"God is our protection and our strength. He always helps in times of trouble."

Psalm 46:1 (NCV)

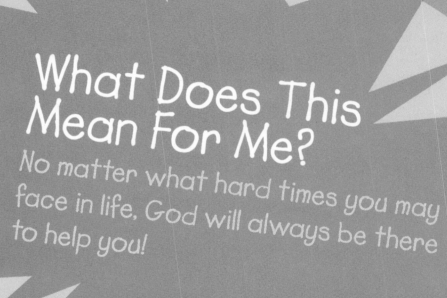

What Does This Mean For Me?

No matter what hard times you may face in life, God will always be there to help you!

God's Promise

"Call to me and I will answer
you and tell you great and
unsearchable things you do
not know."
Jeremiah 33:3 (NIV)

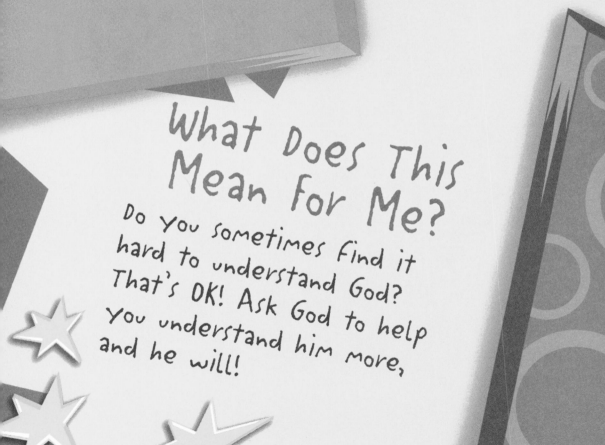

What Does This Mean For Me?

Do you sometimes find it hard to understand God? That's OK! Ask God to help you understand him more, and he will!

God's Promise

"I will be with you always, even until the end of the world."
Matthew 28:20 (CEV)

What Does This Mean For Me?

Jesus will never leave you! Not today, not tomorrow, not ever!

God's Promise

"He will not let you stumble and fall; the one who watches over you will not sleep."
Psalm 121:3 (NLT)

What Does This Mean For Me?

God is never too tired to watch over and protect you!

God's Promise

"The Lord is near to all who call on him, to all who call on him in truth."
Psalm 145:18 (NIV)

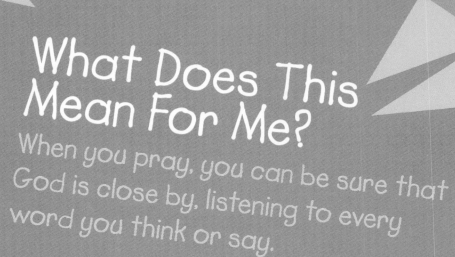

What Does This Mean For Me?

When you pray, you can be sure that God is close by, listening to every word you think or say.

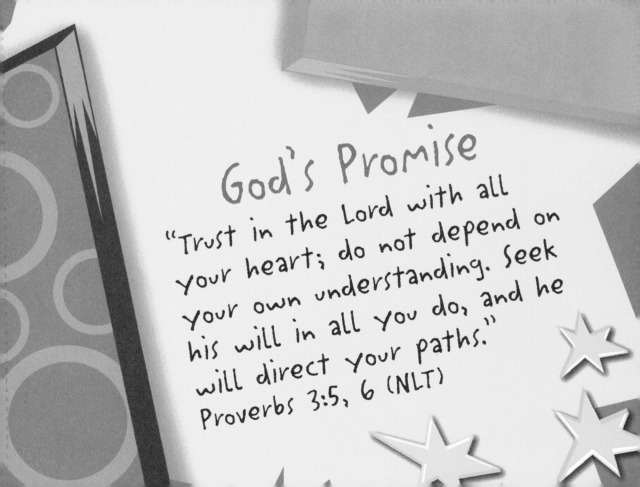

God's Promise

"Trust in the Lord with all your heart; do not depend on your own understanding. Seek his will in all you do, and he will direct your paths."
Proverbs 3:5, 6 (NLT)

What Does This Mean For Me?

God always knows what's best for you. Try to follow his desires for you by reading the Bible for instruction and praying for help and he will help you make good choices in life.

God's Promise

"God cares for you, so turn all your worries over to him."
1 Peter 5:7 (CEV)

What Does This Mean For Me?

When you feel like worrying, remember God cares about you! You can trust him to help you handle all the things you're worried about—even that big test on Friday.

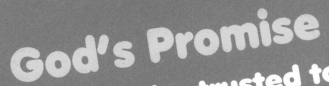

God's Promise

"The Lord can be trusted to make you strong and protect you from harm."
2 Thessalonians 3:3 (CEV)

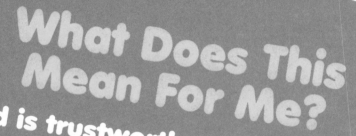

What Does This Mean For Me?

God is trustworthy! If you ask him to help you, he will give you strength and protect you!

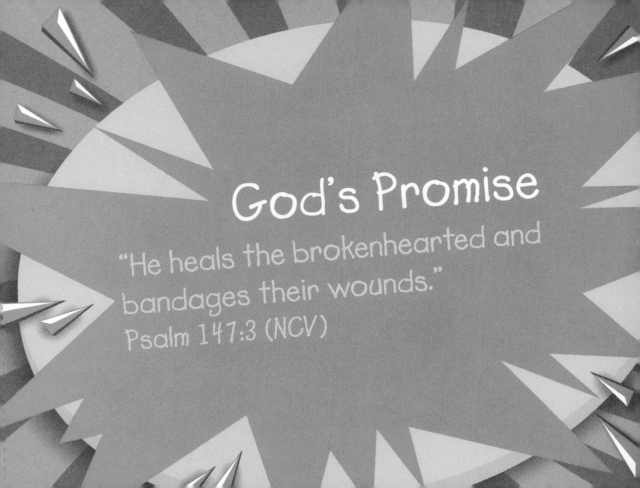

God's Promise

"He heals the brokenhearted and
bandages their wounds."
Psalm 147:3 (NCV)

What Does This Mean For Me?

When you feel very sad, you can turn to God and pray. He always cares for you, and will help to ease your sadness so you can begin feeling better.

God's Promise

"Those who hope in the Lord will renew their strength. They will soar on wings like eagles; they will run and not grow weary, they will walk and not be faint."

Isaiah 40:31 (NIV)

What Does This Mean For Me?

Sometimes it's hard to wait and hope for God's help to come, but if you refuse to give up on God, he will give you amazing strength to keep on living for him.

God's Promise

"People who do what is right may have many problems, but the Lord will solve them all."

Psalm 34:19 (NCV)

What Does This Mean For Me?

Believing in Jesus doesn't mean you will never have problems. It does mean that God will always help you deal with them.

God's Promise

"So don't worry, because I am with you. Don't be afraid, because I am your God. I will make you strong and will help you; I will support you with my right hand that saves you."
Isaiah 41:10 (NCV)

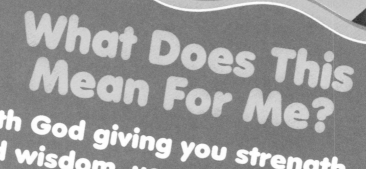

What Does This Mean For Me?

With God giving you strength and wisdom, you can face any problem in life—and overcome it!

God's Promise

"The Lord is my light and my salvation—whom shall I fear? The Lord is the stronghold of my life—of whom shall I be afraid?"
Psalm 27:1 (NIV)

What Does This Mean For Me?

When God is on your side, you don't have to be afraid of anyone or anything!

God's Promise

"Praise the Lord, I tell myself, and never forget the good things he does for me. He forgives all my sins and heals all my diseases."
Psalm 103:2, 3 (NLT)

What Does This Mean For Me?

Praise God! He does wonderful things for us! He forgives us when we do wrong, and even has the power to heal us when we are sick.

God's Promise

"If any of you need wisdom, you should ask God, and it will be given to you. God is generous and won't correct you for asking."

James 1:5 (CEV)

What Does This Mean For Me?

When you need to know what is right and what is wrong, ask God! God loves to give to you and is glad when you ask him for help.

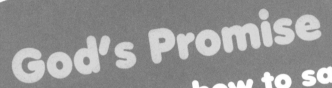

God's Promise

"The Lord knows how to save those who serve him when troubles come."
2 Peter 2:9 (NCV)

What Does This Mean For Me?

When troubles come in your life, you can trust God to help you. After all, God knows everything, so he surely knows the best way to help you during a hard time!

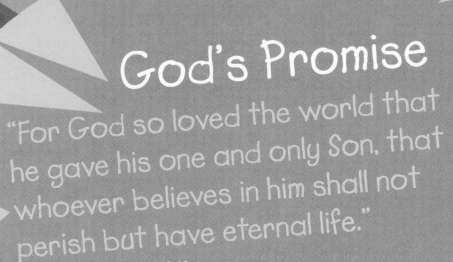

God's Promise

"For God so loved the world that he gave his one and only Son, that whoever believes in him shall not perish but have eternal life."
John 3:16 (NIV)

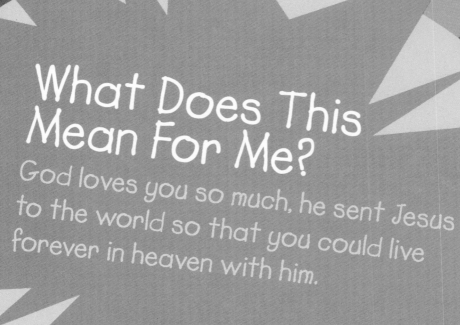

What Does This Mean For Me?

God loves you so much, he sent Jesus to the world so that you could live forever in heaven with him.

God's Promise

"Jesus Christ is the same yesterday and today and forever." Hebrews 13:8 (NIV)

What Does This Mean for Me?

Jesus never changes. He loved you yesterday, he loves you today, and he will still love you tomorrow.

God's Promise

"The Lord is my shepherd; I have everything I need."

Psalm 23:1 (NLT)

What Does This Mean For Me?

Like a shepherd cares for his sheep, God will also care for you and give you everything you need to live your life for him.

God's Promise

"So give yourselves completely to God. Stand against the devil, and the devil will run from you."
James 4:7 (NCV)

What Does This Mean For Me?

Satan will try to lead you away from God and will try to make you do what is wrong. But if you trust in God and refuse to do wrong, the devil will run away from you.

God's Promise

"Don't worry about anything; instead, pray about everything. Tell God what you need, and thank him for all he has done. If you do this, you will experience God's peace, which is far more wonderful than the human mind can understand. His peace will guard your hearts and minds as you live in Christ Jesus."

Philippians 4:6, 7 (NLT)

What Does This Mean For Me?

When you feel like worrying, pray instead! If you do this, God will give you peace of mind and help you overcome your fears.

God's Promise

"Everything and everyone that the Father has given me will come to me, and I won't turn any of them away."
John 6:37 (CEV)

What Does This Mean For Me?

Jesus promises to save everyone who follows him. He will not turn anyone away.

God's Promise

"I tell you for certain that everyone who has faith in me has eternal life."

John 6:47 (CEV)

What Does This Mean For Me?

When you trust Jesus to save you and to lead you in life, he promises that after you die, he will take you to heaven to live forever with him!

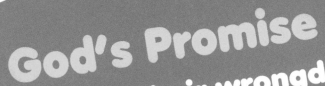

God's Promise

"I will forgive their wrongdoings, and I will never again remember their sins." Hebrews 8:12 (NLT)

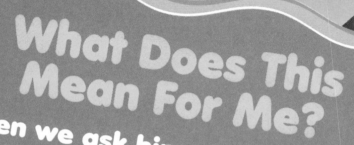

What Does This Mean For Me?

When we ask him, God not only forgives us—he chooses to forget that we ever did something wrong!

God's Promise

"The Spirit we received does not make us slaves again to fear; it makes us children of God. With that Spirit we cry out, 'Father.' And the Spirit himself joins with our spirits to say we are God's children."
Romans 8:15, 16 (NCV)

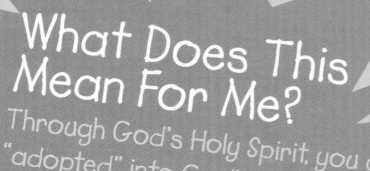

What Does This Mean For Me?

Through God's Holy Spirit, you can be "adopted" into God's family. Then you become God's child, and he becomes your Father—the greatest Dad of all!

God's Promise

"I am still confident of this: I will see the goodness of the Lord in the land of the living."

Psalm 27:13 (NIV)

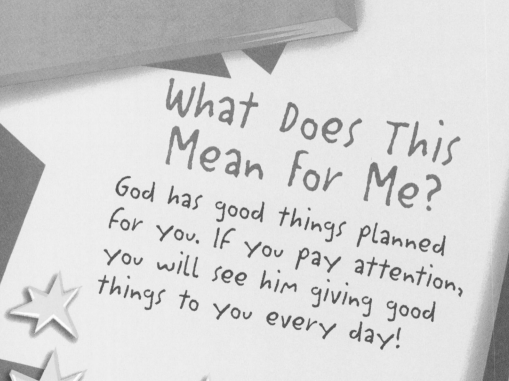

What Does This Mean For Me?

God has good things planned for you. If you pay attention, you will see him giving good things to you every day!

God's Promise

"I lift up my eyes to the hills—
where does my help come from?
My help comes from the Lord, the
Maker of heaven and earth."

Psalm 121:1, 2 (NIV)

What Does This Mean For Me?

When you need help with a problem, ask God for help! He made heaven and earth; he can surely help make a solution to your problem as well!

God's Promise

"You, Lord, give true peace to those who depend on you, because they trust you."
Isaiah 26:3 (NCV)

What Does This Mean For Me?

When you feel tense or afraid—maybe your family is fighting or you feel like you've got more homework than you can finish on time—you can ask God to help calm your fears and bring peace to your heart. He will give you peace!

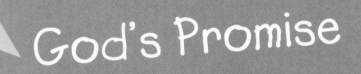

God's Promise

"We know that God causes everything to work together for the good of those who love God and are called according to his purpose for them."
Romans 8:28 (NLT)

What Does This Mean For Me?

Even though bad things will happen in your life, you can trust that God will use every situation you face to bring about something good for you.

God's Promise

"There are many rooms in my Father's home, and I am going to prepare a place for you."
John 14:2, 3 (NLT)

What Does This Mean For Me?

Right now, this very minute, Jesus is preparing a wonderful place for you in heaven! What do you think it's like?

God's Promise

"For I am convinced that neither death nor life, neither angels nor demons, neither the present nor the future, nor any powers, neither height nor depth, nor anything else in all creation, will be able to separate us from the love of God that is in Christ Jesus our Lord."

Romans 8:38, 39 (NIV)

What Does This Mean For Me?

Thanks to Jesus, there's nothing that can keep you from experiencing God's great love for you!

God's Promise

"God loves the person who gives cheerfully. And God will generously provide all you need. Then you will always have everything you need and plenty left over to share with others."
2 Corinthians 9:7, 8 (NLT)

What Does This Mean For Me?

God loves for people to happily give what they have to others. And when you give to others, God will always be giving to you as well. He'll give you so much that you'll have more to keep giving away!

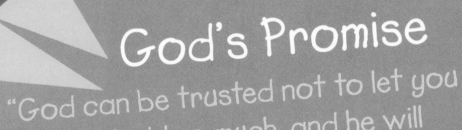

God's Promise

"God can be trusted not to let you be tempted too much, and he will show you how to escape from your temptations."
1 Corinthians 10:13 (CEV)

What Does This Mean For Me?

You will sometimes be tempted to do what is wrong, but you don't have to give in to that temptation! That's because God promises to never let you face a temptation that's too strong for you! He will give you strength and a way out.

God's Promise

"Anyone who calls on the Lord will be saved."
Romans 10:13 (NCV)

What Does This Mean For Me?

If you ask Jesus to forgive your sins and to lead you through the rest of your life—he will!

God's Promise

"With God all things are possible."

Mark 10:27 (NKJV)

What Does This Mean For Me?

God can do anything! Even when you think something is impossible, God can always help you, no matter what!

God's Promise

"My grace is enough for you.
When you are weak, my power
is made perfect in you."
2 Corinthians 12:9 (NCV)

What Does This Mean For Me?

Even though you feel small, God can use you! In fact, the smaller or weaker you feel, the more God can show his power through you!

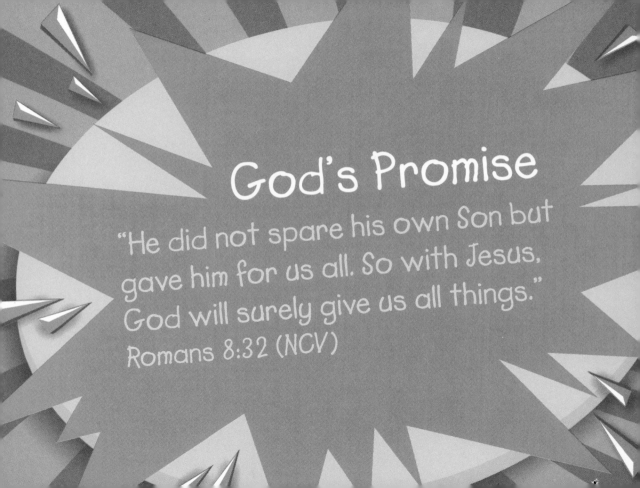

God's Promise

"He did not spare his own Son but gave him for us all. So with Jesus, God will surely give us all things."
Romans 8:32 (NCV)

What Does This Mean For Me?

God loves you so much, he gave his Son, Jesus, for you. If God would give that much for you, he will surely give you everything else you may need to live and to follow him each day.

God's Promise

"Jesus said, 'Don't let your hearts be troubled. Trust in God, and trust in me.'"
John 14:1 (NCV)

What Does This Mean For Me?

When you feel stressed, sad, or frightened, you can trust Jesus to help you!

God's Promise

"Crying may last for a night, but joy comes in the morning."
Psalm 30:5 (NCV)

What Does This Mean For Me?

There are sad things that happen in this world, and everyone goes through times when they feel sad. When you trust God, you know that sooner or later God will bring joy back into your life, and your sadness can end.

God's Promise

"So, my dear brothers and sisters, be strong and steady, always enthusiastic about the Lord's work, for you know that nothing you do for the Lord is ever useless."
1 Corinthians 15:58 (NLT)

What Does This Mean For Me?

Even the smallest thing you do for God matters—helping your mom with the dishes or bringing just one friend to church. So never give up on serving him each day.

God's Promise

"God does not see the same way people see. People look at the outside of a person, but the Lord looks at the heart."
1 Samuel 16:7 (NCV)

What Does This Mean For Me?

God looks at what's inside you. He sees who you really are and doesn't judge you because of what you look like or wear.

God's Promise

"The Lord searches all the earth for people who have given themselves completely to him. He wants to make them strong."

2 Chronicles 16:9 (NCV)

What Does This Mean For Me?

God knows when you follow and serve him. He will make you strong to be able to serve him well!

God's Promise

"Commit to the Lord whatever you do, and your plans will succeed."
Proverbs 16:3 (NIV)

What Does This Mean For Me?

Pray and ask God to help you do the good things that are part of his plan for you. When you do this, he will help you to succeed in doing good!

God's Promise

"God will wipe away every tear from their eyes; there shall be no more death, nor sorrow, nor crying. There shall be no more pain, for the former things have passed away."
Revelation 21:4 (NKJV)

What Does This Mean For Me?

Heaven, the place that God is preparing for all who believe in him, will be a wonderful place! God himself will be there, and he will take away all that is bad so that we can truly live happily ever after!